From a Grey Mouse to a Proud One

-Create your own unique business identity using the 'Fortune-teller Model'

By G.L.Everine Johansen

ALL RIGHTS RESERVED. This book contains material protected under International and Federal Copyright Laws and Treaties. Any unauthorized reprint or use of this material is prohibited. No part of this book may be reproduced or transmitted in any form or by any means, electronic or mechanical, including photocopying, recording, or by any information storage and retrieval system without express written permission from the author / publisher.

From a Grey Mouse to a Proud One
-Create your own unique business identity using the 'Fortune-teller Model'

Copyright©2022; G.L.Everine Johansen

ISBN : 978-1-716-03026-0

Imprint Lulu.com

Intro

Sorry about that title. I don't wish to say that it is something wrong with your business as it is now. That is not my intention. I would have called it *"Stand Out"*, but that title is already taken thanks to Marcus Buckingham. (Great book by the way and well worth a read.) The title is more to do with the feeling you get that your business is blending into the background. Where you wish you could be a bit more visible, but don't know how.

Beginning to create an identity for your business helps you to think things through. Where you have been and where you want to go from here. Taking initiative to the process and work through it also gives you self-respect and a sense of ownership.

This book is to inspire you to see that you and your' business can be someone too. It is not about pretending to be someone you are not, but more to create an identity that fits your business using your shop as a starting point. An identity that in the end you can relate to and be proud of because you created it.

How do you begin when you want

to start all over?

When?

Contents

WHERE YOU ARE NOW 9
    AVOIDING THE BUSINESS LIFE CYCLE 12
        Introducing new products or services 41
    PARTIALLY CHANGING YOUR SHOP 47

THE FORTUNE-TELLER MODEL 57
    CONNECTING THE DOTS 63
    ADDING THAT EXTRA 95

EVALUATION 101

PROJECT PLANNING 109
    PROJECT PLANNING DETAILS 115

A WORD AT THE END 121

Where you are now

Maybe your business is going well. Or it goes, sort of. You manage somehow, anyway and you picked up this book in a half-inspired whim. It doesn't hurt to read about it and your favourite magazine was sold out. It's fine, I am not offended. Books about business-identity are flooding and it is not exactly a new theme. Well, this one is a bit different and it is going to shake you up a bit. (Or a lot if you want to.) Changing your business completely is most likely to be your last resort and even when its un-mistakably heading for a closure you want to hang on to the way it is for as long as possible. It is nothing unusual in that, it feels safe knowing what you got. Making changes can be scary and besides it takes money and energy, both which you haven't got at the moment. Okay, so you don't want to make any changes and you are lukewarm to this business identity thing. That's fine, but after reading this book you may *want* to change it because you have an idea of where your business is heading.

Let me point out that finding your business identity here is first and foremost a mental stretch that we play with on paper. Creating your business identity and the implementation of it are two separate parts and the implementation of it doesn't have to come straight after the other. Give yourself space to work with it and plan it. Then when the time is right you are ready to put it into action.

What is a business identity anyway?

Hey, don't you skip this page. Yes, yes, I know you have heard it all before. Differentiate your business by creating a brand and use marketing to create positive associations. What do you want your business to be associated with and so on and so on. I am pretty sick of it too and if any of you mention a logo you get a punishment of a ten minutes run. Or in these days, ten laps around your coach. For me this is all glazing, outer appearance, superficial gloss. How on earth are you supposed to create a brand out of nowhere? Where do you start? It is not easy is it. And making a slogan reminds me of those big companies where they have something nice to appear behind the name and no-one who works there knows what it is because it doesn't have any practical significance anyway. (Ok, I promise I have shorter sentences than that one..)

For me creating a business identity goes deeper than that. Once you changed your business and created a proper identity, creating a brand with a slogan if you want comes easy. That is, if it is necessary at all. (Ask my sister, her pub goes like a rocker without any fancy brand and a slogan.)

If you want to create your business identity the old-fashion way you can, of course, it is totally up to you. Want to try it? Ok, here it goes: You usually read something like differentiate yourself by enhancing what is unique about your business.

So, have a think about this:

What is unique about your' business?

Let that simmer while reading on.

It can be difficult to start so I am going to help you along a bit. Here are some identity-clues:

-*What do you sell, do you sell something different?*

-*Location?*

-*History of the shop?*

-*Atmosphere in the shop?*

-*Friendly staff?*

-*You; do you stand out from the crowd?*

You may have an inkling of a business identity after this. How many of you wanted to go ahead and make that brand without changing anything in the shop? Tempting, isn't it. Identity is about creating a whole, meaning if your shop is full of contradictions it doesn't feel right. Do the colour scheme and the interior match what you sell? Does it fit the type of customers you have in mind?

Does what your sell goes together?

After you looked at that, pick one of the identity-clues that go best with what you sell. A little word of advice, try not to hang your identity on a service. It can easily be pinched by your competitors and then where you do you stand?

Now create a slogan that represents it. (Not that easy, right?)

Take a look at your shop. Does your shop reflect the identity-clue you picked and your slogan? If you feel frustrated at this point, you are not alone and it is one of the reasons I am writing this book.

Can I ask you something, do you now feel like you actually have a business identity?

Avoiding the Business Life Cycle

- **About the Business Life Cycle and its' phases.**

I know, I know, this is about creating a business identity and we will get to that eventually. (Or you could just skip right to it.) But before we get to that it is best to think a few things through. A mental preparation if you like.

'Avoiding the Business Life Cycle' is if you want to have a go and improve your business before making any major changes. It is also to support you when things are changing along the way. After all, running a business is a dynamic and organic process. It is describing different phases a business goes through and what you can do in each of them.

Recently I watched the news and it was about a paper mill called *Norske Skog* (means Norwegian Forest.) and how it was saved from closure, yet again. It always puts a smile on my face when I read about them and I have nicknamed them the Phoenix. They have risen from the ashes and been saved from closure so many times over the years that I have lost count.

You may have heard about the business life cycle where a business has its' beginning and its' end and a peak in-between. When you think that this is true and you hit a rough spot, which frankly can be quite often, thoughts like "is *this it then, have I passed the peak and hit the inevitable closure*" can easily crop up. You can even get this advice from experts that oh, well, perhaps it is your time it is quite old or the days of these types of businesses are over and so on.

What is a business life cycle anyway?

A business life cycle is described in terms similar to a product life-cycle. In *Marketing Management* written by *Philip Kotler, (co-writer Kevin Lane Keller)* published by *Prentice Hall, 2009* it is described liked this:

"Product Life cycles

Most product life cycle curves are portrayed as bell-shaped. This curve is typically divided into four stages: introduction, growth, maturity, and decline."

I like to challenge this notion that when a business is seemingly dead without any customers, the only way forward is closure. The example of the paper mill is a living proof of that.
The trouble is when your mind is fixed on thinking in terms of a life cycle you can risk creating a self-fulfilling prophesy. You may not even be aware that you do, this thinking can be in your subconscious as a hidden truth. It is a chance that you have misread the situation. That in reality you can actually change your situation and come out on top, but because you have a mind-set where you have already given up you don't search for solutions. Neither sees them when they turn up. By just sitting and wait for doomsday the doomsday will come. I am trying to help you with this and change the image we are carrying in our mind. Try to think of your business-situation in terms of phases. Instead of the ups and downs, just different phases you are going through.

Back to the example of the paper mill, they have switched between the success phase and the funeral phase many times, only a few times been in the maintenance. That is why they make me smile because one day you can read about them having a success and the next it is doom and gloom only to re-appear reporting it is all a success again. They are still hanging in there and have done so for years despite of being on the brink of closure several times. Perhaps this is more typical for the industry they are in than the average retail shop, but still it shows that it is possible.

The Phases

The Phases are descriptions of different phases a business goes through in its daily life and in its life-spam.

The Business Phases

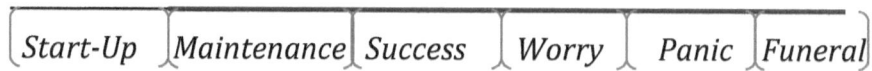

-(Start-Up – not described here)
-The maintenance
-The success
-The worry
-The panic
-The funeral

I am describing the different phases in a downward spiral from the beginning to the end as in the business life cycle, but I am afraid I have tricked you a bit. In real life it doesn't happen like that.

You can go from start-up and straight to the funeral. Or you can easily find yourself switching between them and more often than not, you are in a mix of them. The length of the different phases can also vary and vary from time to time.

The Maintenance

Already in the title it differs from the business life-cycle. Here *the Maintenance* comes before *the Success* phase or growth as it is called in the life cycle. *Maintenance* comes after the start-up phase where you have reached stability in form of a steady income and daily routines.

Here you can either be at peace with how things are and not thinking about how your business is going. Just getting up and going to work and have more or less monotonous days. Or you can be a bit, if not worried but preoccupied with keeping things as they are and not wanting to change things in case you ruin everything.
Either way it is easy to get caught up in the comfort of it or the thought of wanting to keep things at is it. You don't have to make major changes, but at least think things through or try something new. This helps you stand stronger when changes come.

Now you are in a position where you can use the opportunity to ask yourself some question without having the immediate pressure of money and time.

Try to make a detail list as possible over what products and services constitute your steady income.

Does anything surprise you?

- Which ones are services, which ones are products?

-Is one part bigger than the other or are they equally distributed?

-Which ones are complementary products and which ones are "main" products?

-Are there only old products that sell or are there any new ones in the mix?

Description of the steady income

Describe product #	M	C	O	N
1				
2				
3				
Describe the service #				
1				
2				

Set an X where it fits

M= Main product
C= Complementary product
O= Old product
N= New product

The Success

This phase is best described as having more than enough money where you spend most of your time managing and organizing. Or should I say you are running your heals off trying to stay on top of everything.

First thing you can do is to try to get an overview over your situation. In this phase it is so easy to lose the overview and I think it is rarer to have the overview than not.

In the *Maintenance* you look at what product or service that sells. Her you include customer clusters in the mix and try to get an overview of who is buying what.

Okay so you make more money, but where do they come from? What sells best? Is it the old products that were your steady income stream that has suddenly gotten an up-lift? Or is it a completely new product that has taken off? To clarify, when I say a completely new product that has taken off, I mean a product in your shop that didn't sold before. Or is it an external product, a seasonal product perhaps that you just taken in? Or is it a mix of two or all three?

Who is buying them? Is it your regular customers who is buying more or is it new customers? Or is it random, seasonal customers?

Product and Customer Overview

Product type **Customer type**	Old products	New products	External products
Regular customers			
New customers			
Random, seasonal customers			

Regular Customers

Old products
Regular customers buying old products mean the same customers are buying more of the same products they bought before. Is this new increase in income and buying pattern big enough to consider focusing only on these products as in becoming more specialized? Why this buying pattern, why do they buy more of these products? What's behind it? Is it new hobbies, if so can you expand on it and offer more products in line with that? Regular customers are gold so it is worth working on keeping them. Are there ways you can give them extra treats? Perhaps a membership- club? Try to find out what they want more of and figure out a way to meet their needs.

New products
It can be worrying when your regular customers begin to buy new products. Especially when they deviate from their normal buying pattern and you get a drop in number of purchases in what they usually buy. When this happens try not to worry, it is natural to be interested in buying new things when you get tired of the old ones and just want to try something new for a change. Let it happen instead of panic and try to push them into the old products; which will have the opposite effect. It is better to sit back and let it happen and push the new products they are buying. However, it is worth keeping an eye on it.

Try to figure out why this happens and if it is a current trend or if it is a long term change. Have they stopped buying what they used to buy all together? If so, for how long? Can you figure out why? Did something occur at a specific time?

What new products are they buying? Is it something completely different or is it tied in with what they bought before? Can you take in more products that are in line with the new products they are buying?

Of, course it is a question when do you switch.

Do you let the old products just be and increase the amount you order of the new products? Or do you pack away the old products and fully focus on the new products?

You can experience that after a while your customers come asking for the old products and you have taken them out of stock, which is the fear of the shop-keeper. That is why it is a bit important to dig around and figure out why they are buying these new products. If it is only a trend they might want to go back to the old products when they are done with the new. If it is a bigger change such as a change in the way of living or thinking then the chances are the pattern of buying these new products will stay.

Think about this:

-How much money are you making from the sale of these new products in comparison to what you earned before, from the sale of the old products? Are you making more or less? If less, when is your tipping point? Meaning look at your figures and see how long this can go on before you have to initiate actions to increase your revenue.

External product
When regular customers buy a new, external product it is a good thing because this means they come more often to your shop.

Work *with* this when this happens and see if you can complement the external product with products from your shop. What products do you have that goes well with it? How many combinations can you think of? Is it a product that you can include in your stock in a more daily basis? Has this product a potential of becoming a new, steady income or is it more a short-term interest? Are there other external products you can take in that goes well with it?

New Customers

Old products
When most of your income comes from new customers buying old products it is an interesting and concerning setting at the same time. Interesting because this shows that your products are not out of date and concerning because the question is what happened to your usual, regular customers? Why did they fade out? Or did most of them stop coming at the same time? Try to think back to see if you can find a reason why this change in customers. New customers buying old products mean they haven't yet become your regulars. What can you do to make them want to come back? What are they buying most of?
What do they need, any difference in the need of your previous regular customers?

Try to get an overview of who exactly your new customers are. Where do they live, are they local or commuting? What age? Can you see any clusters, such as in a sport club or organization etc? This information can help you decide how to market the products and what new products you can take in. Perhaps some of them knows one of your previous regular customers and got interested that way?

New products
When new customers buy new products it is a clear indication of a new trend. New products here don't mean new as in recently entered the market. It means products in your shop that haven't sold that much before. Did some of your customers make the transition from buying old products to this new? If so, why and how many of them did that? New customers coming in and buying one of your products that up until now haven't sold that much means something is moving in the market. Does this mean you can drop the other products and turn around and hang everything on these new products? No, as usual try to dig a bit more. Why this sudden upswing in the sale of these products? Is this a short trend or is it part of a bigger, long lasting change in the society? Or is it a local phenomenon?

External products
New customers buying external products mean you have a steady flow of customers. The downside is they are not buying your products. External products means say you have a clothes shop and people come and buy the new clothes you have ordered because they are popular in general. You see them in magazines, blogs, news, other shops etc. Or it could be an item you want to sell because you know it is a best seller elsewhere.

Try to get them to see your products as well and try to connect what you are selling with these external products. The difficulty here is what do you do when these external products are completely different from what you are selling?

Do you adjust and change to follow these products? Which is quite tempting, but it does mean in the end to change into a different type of shop altogether.

You can take in some products that go well with these external products and that way ease the way in a bit.

Another way is to find out what other interests the customers have. Meaning your products might meet other needs they have, needs that these external products doesn't meet.

No matter if it is old, new or external products when your biggest income comes from new customers it is mostly about trying to get them to come back and become a regular.

Random and seasonal customers

I heard you, and no, I don't mean only tourists.
It also includes people that show up only when you offer the products for a specific season or they are mainly drop-ins that pop in only to buy one or two specific items while on their way to another designation.

Finding yourself in this category you have your work cut out.
You can have regular customers, but they tend to be less loyal and the overall focus is on the products itself and not so much the products, your shop and you as a package.

This in turn puts a pressure on keeping up with the market in terms of having products up to date and a more aggressive line with marketing. If you are comfortable with that, then no problem. It is all fine when it goes well. An increase in sales here means you have an increase in the flow of customers and an increase in the number of sale at the same time. When the sale plummets here it can be sudden and uncomfortable.

Think about this

-It can be just as challenging to try to keep them being a regular as in trying to get new customers in. Weigh those up against each other and see what you are most comfortable with and what you are best at.

Old products, new products and external products

Whether you sell mostly of your old products, the new products or external ones doesn't really matter when most of your customers are random and seasonal.
The focus here is on the products and why they buy them. Customers here come to your shop not necessarily because they are loyal to you. They come because they know they can buy these specific products there or that it is of a good quality, it is cheap or both.
Try to find out why they buy the products at your shop and not somewhere else. Is it one of the reasons above? Perhaps it is a completely different one such as it is convenient or the name of your shop is easy to remember.

Think about this

-Can you think of a catch-phrase to use to capture the essence of your shop? What is the most important thing you want to inform them about?

A little PS!

Working with the progress

I know that in this period, in this *Success* phase, you are advised to work with the progress. This means using the success to your advantage by trying to speed it up even more and take it to the next level. To do that it means even more work and you have to have the capacity to follow it up. You don't just sling something out there randomly and expect it to take care of itself. What you can do however that gives you the least amount of work in form of following it up is to attach it to something that already sells best.

Working through the form *Product and Customer Overview* helps you to do just that.

Be careful and align and direct the success with your business identity. If not you can find that after the wave of the success is gone you have a different business before it started. You can get the feeling that the control of your business has been taken out of your hand and you have to follow it up; even if you don't identify with it anymore. Losing the feeling of connection to your business is more dangerous than you think. You lose the sense of ownership; it doesn't feel like it belongs to you anymore.

The Worry

This phase is a difficult one because you spend most of your time in your head. The nagging feeling of being worried is constantly with you and the question if you should do something or not isn't going away.
Being in the *Worry* phase it feels like you have been transported into some narrow movie. You know, the one where you own a train-station in the middle of nowhere and a few odd looking people sitting on the benches waiting. That's the feeling you have when you are in this phase. It feels odd.

Almost as if you accidently dropped into a time-capsule where everything stands still and you get dragged into the same energy. In a weird way it can be a comfort.

It is not easy to know what to do here. What do you do? Can you picture yourself getting the customers you have left all geared up and excited about a new product or event? Can you get excited? Exactly.
Getting out of this energy isn't going to be easy.

Here your daily routine becomes your comfort. It is something to hold on to when things are uncertain. Keep them. If you find them comforting, then good. On bad days they can be the only thing that holds you together.

Another worry you carry with you is the one about your old customers. They are regular customers that have been faithful for years and you feel you owe it to them to remain the same. Questions like *"What would happen to them? What would they do? I can't do that to them."* pops up into mind. You feel guilty when you want to make changes.

What you can do is to sort of let them be and find ways to serve them and take care of them as usual.

Options:

A) Going back

Think back to a time where you had success and the shop was full of people.

What has changed in your shop since then? Can you recreate it?

Can you pick one or two things that were the reason for your success? How can you emphasize it and make it better?

B) Work with it

What you can do is instead of trying to enliven things up work with this slow energy. Make your business into a slow business.

What do you think of when you hear the word slow?

It can be about taking your time to enjoy something say food. The something here has to be connected to your business in some way.

Can you connect it to a specific era?

Or perhaps a genre in movies?

Or make it a historic building?

C) Go Personal

What are you interested in? Do you have any hobbies you can integrate in your business? What can you teach; can you hold any courses in a subject?

D) Events

If you have the space you can arrange events in your shop.

What activities can you do in the shop? What would be natural for your type of shop? What activities could attract new customers?

If you don't have the space then you could arrange an event on behalf of the shop? As in if you sell sports equipment and outdoor clothes perhaps a charity run or a Thursday walk?

This slow period could be a part of the natural ups and downs of having a business.

To find that out ask these questions:

-Is there a drop in the economy, unemployment rate has gone up, people have little money or people simply have gone off it for a while, wanting a change etc.?

-Have your products been replaced by something in the market, leaving your products superfluous?

-Have any new competitors popped up in your neighbourhood or perhaps online?

A Simple Business Plan

Being in the *Worry* phase is a bit like being in a limbo. You are doing something while you are deciding on what to do.
You have lost your identity.

This is the time to figure out what you actually want to do, both with your business and your life in general.

In the original book I placed the business-plan in the *Success* phase because I thought it would help to get an overview of the situation and help with the planning. It seems though that the business-plan is more useful here, in the *Worry* phase. When your head is full of worrying thoughts it is difficult to think straight. Going through the business-plan helps you to think clearer and to see what you can and want to do.

After you worked through the business-plan you can continue and work with the *'Fortune-teller Model'* and see what you find out.

Should everyone in this phase re-invent their business? No, but it doesn't hurt to have a solid business identity. Then you know better what actions to take because they would be aligned with the identity.

Business-plan Form

What- What business do you want to have? What do you want to sell? Write a short statement describing your business.	
Why – Why do you want to do this? What reasons and thoughts are behind it?	
Who – Who do you want to offer it to?	
How – How do you plan to sell it?	
You- What interests and talents do you get to use in this? What are you longing for? What do you wish you could do more of? How can you utilize your abilities in your business?	

The Panic

The *Worry* phase is distinct by the lack of action. Here in the *Panic* phase it is the opposite. This is where you go straight from one idea to the next without thinking it through properly.

The *Panic* phase can be just as busy as the *Success* and even more stressful, not knowing what would work.
Here it is not only that you can't think straight, you don't think full stop.
The challenge here is to try to connect to your thoughts again. Stop and take a deep breath. Literarily.
The good thing is that you are actually doing something. The bad thing is if you are not careful you can drive your business to the ground quite quickly.
This is about getting out of this frenetic state of mind and making conscious choices.

Stop and step back. Try to get an objective overview of your situation and your options. Feeling and being in a state of panic isn't the same as your business being in one. Objectivity here is the clue.

Establish what type of panic phase you are in. The *Panic* phase can occur with two different scenarios. It can be where you are in the W*orry* phase and even if it is slow at least you have some steady income. Then you get a drop and your situation goes from bad to worse. This is entering the *Panic* phase. The other situation is where you have been in the *Success* phase and where you get a sudden drop in your income and you *think* you are in a bad situation, but in reality it goes back to how it used to be before the success, meaning you are in the *Maintenance* phase.

Once you established you are in the genuine *Panic* phase it is time to look at what you can do and what options are available.

When you are in this phase and you want take action it is easy to think that *"okay, what we have isn't selling so what is popular"?* Adapting to what is popular doesn't have to be right for your shop. That it is popular elsewhere isn't a guarantee that it will sell when you try to do it. If you are unfortunate it can seem odd or out of place. Another common idea to get after this one is *"what is missing in this place, what are people missing?"* I am not saying that these are bad ideas; in fact I have suggested it myself. It is the wrong time to use them, but if you do they have to be put in the context of your shop. Using them wrongly here can ruin your business.

Here we have, or should I say had, a fish-restaurant. Beautiful seated near the shore by a little pier. Perfect for the summer guests who came by boat. They could tie up their boat and walk right in and have a lovely meal. Perfect. Then the pandemic stroked.

What they did was this:

First they had a smashing marketing campaign and landed an awesome coupon deal with the biggest business around here. I have to say, that marketing was absolutely fabulous. (No, irony.) I take my hat off to them regarding the marketing, they were brilliant at that. The marketing campaign aimed towards the local was a smart move since they usually served summer guests. That wasn't the bad bit. The bad bit came after. Since the money didn't came in as fast as they would have liked, they came up with one idea after another. They suddenly announced that they were installing an Italian pizza-oven and serving pizzas. And the week or two after that an interview in the newspaper said they were hiring a chef and offered a-la-carte menu with dishes you'd seen in the 80`.

(If you know of examples from where you live I love to hear about them. I promise I do better finding examples from other places in my next book.)

What would you have done?

I can't say that I would have done anything differently from them. It is easy for me as an outsider to say in hindsight what they should have done. Because that is the problem, when you are in the middle of it you don't think straight.
And yes, yesterday I read the announcement that they were bankrupt.

What can you do then, what other ways are there?

-Make a speciality
Take a look around your shop. Any item(s) you think would be great to single out?

What item would you like your shop to be known for?

Anything you can make yourself?

Take a look at the news, blogs, and your local area. What item do you think would be appropriate and popular? (Read, putting it in context.)

-Make a concept
Think in terms of using all of the options at the same time and see if you can combine all of them into one idea.
Is it possible to make a concept out of it? Now what is this concept again? Okay, I use another word, a package, connecting other items to your speciality.

-Go back to your roots
Now it is really not the time to change your business identity. If you have a fish-restaurant as in the previous example then instead of changing it, think of ways to embrace it and enhance it. If you have a clothes-shop take a look at what type of clothes you have. Do you have a bit old-fashioned grandmother type of clothes? Then go all in and think of ways to make it more typical grandmother like.

If you have a convenience store what type of store do you have? Old-fashion? Then think of ways to make it even more old-fashioned. Get my drift?

-Make it easy
Make it easy for people to buy your products and what to buy as well. Set up an online store, offer delivery. Get your products out to people, set up a deal with another shop if they can display your products or set up a stall near crowds, take a van and take it out to places.

-Personal interests
Do you have any personal interests that you can connect to your shop?
Keep in mind that here in the P*anic* phase you need to increase your measures and the impact. Meaning to think a bit bigger. Do you have a convenience store and like cooking or baking? This means thinking wider than baking cakes to sell in your shop, which you can do of course. Think in terms of cooking classes, delivery service, baking for arrangements etc.

The Funeral

I use the word quite deliberately because it feels as though as it is. You are grieving.

Here you don't have any customers at all. There are none.

To figure out what to do next it is important to look at what phase you are coming from. Do you come from the *Success* phase as in the example of the paper mill where the lack of customers is sudden? Or is it more of a slowly dribble as in the *Worry* phase?

If the first is your answer then the sudden drop in customers is more a case of lack of demand. Meaning it is your' products you should focus on. Either you can find other markets for what you are selling, keeping the products as they are. Or you could see if you could find other products to sell to even out this sudden tide. (See the chapter *'Introducing new products or services'*)

Coming from the *Worry* phase where your customers have dwindled away it is time to review the whole business.

Split your focus into two: reviewing your business and getting money in.

Reviewing your business

You may be in a mind-set where you have accepted that they only way forward is closing, but before you do can you look at it again?

What can you do, what options are available?

-Use the options under the *Panic* phase and enlarge them.

a) Renovate
You can do a complete make-over and crisp it up a bit, get a lick of paint, get new furniture and re-shuffle your stuck and then re-launch it. It can work, sometimes people have stopped coming because it looks a bit shabby. Other times it is not enough with a lick of paint and you can risk getting into the same situation you are in now.

b) Create a concept
A concept is to glue your business together. This creates a mix between the old shop and the new.
This can work since it is familiar so people know what it is and at the same time is exciting with the new element.

However, this depends that your type of product is still up-there in the market. Selling outdated products in a new wrapping is not going to work. It is also works against you if you gotten a bad reputation.

c) Create a new identity
You can create a completely new identity using '*The Fortune-teller Model*' here in this book. The downside on this it can take a bit of time and effort, not to mention money. And it takes time before you get an income from the new business identity

d) Personal
Another option is to make it into your personal shop. Pick products that reflects you, choose colours that you like, make displays as you would like. The positive about this one is that it makes you happier by working on it. What do you got to lose? Perhaps though, the last thing you want right now is to give more of yourself.

As you can see there are positive and negative sides with all these options. Only you can tell which one you prefer.

Use this period to think things through about what you really want with your life. (Yes, I know, I said it in the *Worry* phase as well.) Sometimes it is not the business itself you are tired of, but more of the constant lack of money. If you are in doubt try to raise money and see if you feel any differently after you had some money coming in.

 (I also recommend you read through '*When you hate your' business*' which you can find on my website.)

Getting money in temporarily

The actions you do here have to have a bigger impact and be more profound.

-Events
It is not enough to have a sale. You have to make more of it. Make it an event, like an auction for example. Is it possible to make a series of events perhaps with different themes? Take a look at other similar businesses that is a success to see what they have done. Visit them if you can, if not, write to them, call them, look them up online. Ask them for tips.

-Re-invent your products
Is it possible to take your products and use them in a different way or setting? Can you create a new concept out of it?

If you sell clothes you could turn it into a second hand shop and have jumble sales. Or if you are more into re-design you could take the clothes in your shop and re-design them. Do you know any designer who you could invite to re-design one or two clothes which you could sell? If you don't know any designers then think of someone who is known that you could invite to design?

-Hook-it
Are there shops that have a sale campaign going where the products sell well? See if you have any products you can hook on to theirs; as a complementary product.
Say if a hardware store sells electric grills for barbeques. Then you can hook on to their campaign by having a sale campaign yourself and offer products you know would go well to electric grills and barbeques.

-Courses
Do you have any hobbies or specific knowledge that you could combine with your products?

How can you set it up in your shop? (This is to make people get used to come to your shop.)

Connect it to something personal that means something to you. Say if you have a convenience store, love cooking and remember the time you were in Italy. Then you could hold cooking classes with Italian food.

-Investors
I have to mention it because I know you are thinking about it and it is an option. Just be careful though. When someone wants to invest in your business you feel lucky. You might have struggled up front to get people to invest that add to the feeling.

People who put money in your shop when you are in this phase they usually want to take over. At least they will muscle in and tell you how to do things. Coming head to head with them in an argument they use the money against you. Since they have put money in the place, their money they want to add, they mean they have the right to have the last word.
When people want to invest it is better to tie it up to a specific project instead of buying a share in your shop.
Be careful and be clear about this up front and write a contract that is clear to avoid any confusion as well as strengthen your case later on if there should be any disputes. Be aware of the small print.

Well-wishers and gifts can also come in form of other people stepping in and taking over. I mentioned this briefly before. In all phases, but perhaps especially in the *Panic* and here in the *Funeral* phase it is an issue. Dealing with people in this phase is just as much of a problem as your situation itself.

Ask for help for practical things, but be specific. In this phase people have a tendency to take over when you ask for help and when you are exhausted you are inclined to let them. Their attitude doesn't help either and you can get a lot of negative comments. Comments which basically boils down to that you are incompetent and a failure and they would have never done what you have if they have been in charge. I try to restrain my words, but tell them to bugger off. Of, course it is a good idea to get help, but it is has to be you who call the shots. You are good enough and no-one knows your business more than you; no-one. Only you know what will work or not, even if you don't believe so yourself. And if you make a mistake, then at least you will feel it is your own decision. Caving in to those demanding people and it all fails, believe me, they take no responsibility for it; they still blame you.

The *Funeral* phase is the most difficult phase to be in and the longer you are in it the harder it gets.
Your emotions can completely immobilize you. You go numb and get almost in a state of coma; a trance. I won't ask you to "just" snap out of it. I been there myself and I think that comment is rude and show ignorance. But here is the thing. You can't wait for your emotions to catch up before doing anything because that will never happen. You have to let them live their own life and act anyway. Taking action will improve how you feel. In other words, you have to take action while you are in this state. Not an easy task, I know. . The other is that you wait for the perfect solution that will rescue you out of it. I give you a clue; no-one knows for sure what solution will work. It is a gamble; it is in the very nature of the business-world. What you can do is try to put the odds in your favour. Read upon subjects, search online for business-blogs, take notes while reading the news etc. When you have an idea you like evaluate it against what you have found. No-one knows your business better than you and no-one is better qualified to make that decision.

Introducing new products or services

Introducing new products or services is useful when you want to add something new when you feel your business is going a bit slow. You can also use it after you started up with your new business identity. And I don't need to remind you that whatever new products or service you introduce be sure it is in line with your new identity.

Introducing products:

A) Do you want to take in a product that is in line with what you already have and offer more variety?

B) Do you want to take in a product that is almost the same, but in a different version?

C) Or do you want to take in a product that is similar and in line with what you have, but rare?

D) Or do you want to take in a product that is completely different from what you have?

When you want to introduce a new product spend some time doing some research and digging up front. Ask around, ask your friends or family what they miss, and keep your ears open what people are talking about. After you decided what to take in, or even only when you have a vague idea, Google it to get some background information about it.

Do a customer research to try to find out why people come to your shop and what their favourite product is. You can be surprised why people shop where they do. A branch of convenience stores thought they were being clever and wanted to reframe their' image. A part of that was to cut back on some of their stock to save money and take in more of the locally produced products. They thought they did a good thing and looked at the removed products as minor details. It created an uproar, to put it mildly. It turned out that some only came to that shop because they had that particular soda, others because of that type of jam etc. People went to the neighbouring convenience store instead where they had their favourite products. This meant that they lost the customers' dinner and weekend shopping as well. They lost millions nation-wide. Try to spend some time before you decide which product to take in. It is time well spend.

Introducing complementary products:

What product can you sell that goes well with what you sell the most of? What would enhance what you are already selling? If your best selling product is a coffee-machine then a complementary product that would enhance it could be chocolate, category 1. What product can you sell that goes well with what you sell best and at the same sell well on its' own? Using the example of a coffee-machine it could be a milk-steamer or a coffee-grinder, category 2. It is higher up because it cost more, it can stand on its' own and is compatible with the coffee-machine.

Going further with the example of the coffee-machine low level complementary product that goes well with both the coffee-machine and the coffee-grinder could be coffee-beans, category 3.

Then there is the fourth, the accessories that enhances both products and/or help promote it as a package. Of, course you could use the chocolate as in the ex. in category one, but it doesn't help to sell the coffee-machine, the coffee-grinder and the coffee-beans as a packet. You could argue and say that they already are a packet. Sure, but here it is about finding that little extra that lifts it. The dot over the i if you like.

If you buy a coffee-machine, a coffee-grinder and coffee-beans you are really into coffee aren't you. So what would make the coffee even better? It could be filters or different tastes you could add. The ideal is to have products in all four quarters.

Complementary Product Chart	
1. Complementary product to enhance what sells best.	2. Complementary product that can stand on its' own and have potential to make a high income.
3. Low level complementary product that goes well with the products in category 1 and 2, but is at a lower cost.	4. Accessories or other elements that goes well with the products in category 1, 2 and 3 and would make it possible to sell as a package.

Introducing services:

Maybe you can't think of services you can offer. Perhaps you also think that your business isn't the type that will suit with any services. If you do, try to think of these questions:

A) What does your customers might consider as a snag?

How can you remove it or make things easier for them?

B) What would they consider to be that little extra you can offer?

C) Do other shops charge extra for a service you can offer for free or at a reduced price?

Where I live there is a bric-a- brac shop owned until last year, by a little old lady. I probably come back to her several times, because she never stops to fascinate me. By bric- a- brac shop I mean a knick-knack shop, where you can find a little bit of everything. She reminds me of *Aunty Wainwright* in '*Last of the Summer Wine*' played by *Jean Alexander*. It was a long running British TV-series. Look it up if you don't know what I mean, it is well worth the bother. She kept it going for years by offering services, that little extra that other shops didn't have. She had this knack for sensing when a customer was hesitating and offered that little extra service that made it tilt in her favour. She could come and measure your windows so you could get the right size for your curtains, she sew them for you and if you left your key under the door-mat she hung them up for you as well. If you wanted to buy a piece of furniture she could deliver it for free and have her husband carry it in for you, and assemble it as well if you couldn't do it yourself. (The bigger franchise next door charged fifty pound for it or 30-40 U.S.dollars)

When you want to attract new customers try to come up with one that other shops don't have. Shops who already have many customers can offer "common" services as the little extra.

D) You want to offer something new in your shop; does it have to be a product or service?

-Maybe the key here is to offer something new, the little change?

-What little new can you offer that isn't a product or service?

-What little change can you do with what you got?

-Try to think a little bit abstract. What about the times/when you are open?

A little convenience store here lost out to the bigger and central ones. Their' prices on the food were a bit higher as well. It had an extension where you could buy wood, tools and such, you know, everything for the hobby-carpenter. Then they decided to open it up really early. Why? They figured out that the one coming there to buy were men, men who wanted to get cracking by the light of dawn. Did it work? To put it this way, now they expanded the extension and the men are queuing up when it opens. The clever bit they did were they opened up the convenience-store as well at the same time, so the men who came to buy bits and pieces they needed for their' carpentry, bought groceries there too.

Partially changing your shop

Partially changing your shop is about *physically* changes you want to make to your shop. Reading through this before you work through the *'Fortune-teller Model'* gives you a foundation so you have a better inkling of what ideas will work or not. It also can help you to get more ideas because you know what you can physically do with your shop.

There are several options when you partially want to change your business. It is not that one option is better than the other, nor do you have to settle for only one.

☐   - Current size

▨   - Size of the partially change

●   - High income rate/ high in rate of return

A) *The & after your shop's name*

The main idea here is equality. It is the fish after the chips, if you get my drift. This actually is not a bad example when it comes to equality because they both support each other and you can buy them separately. Keep that in mind when you think about what you want to expand with. Unlike a hot dog where the bread doesn't make any sense without the sausage and visa -versa. (Sorry about the food comparison, I think am hungry...) The first is a two way expansion and the other a one way. Meaning the fish and chips you can buy separately and they make sense on their own, whereas in the hot-dog example the sausage and the bread are complementary products to each other. This means how many bread you sell is depending on how many hot dogs you sell. In the first they are two separate units working together which makes it more flexible for you to adjust them later. In the latter they are two objects working together as one unit and only work as one unit. This means if you want to expand you have to expand the whole unit. In the first you can adjust the individual objects separately because they work as a unit on their own.

Another thing to consider:

Keep the word after the & simple. Simple in terms of amount of words and not complicated ones. It is an advantage if people get what you are selling without using a dictionary. Use one word after the & and focus on one expansion at time. I have seen shops where they have gone mad with the names after the &.

Is it necessary to change the name of the shop? Would it make a difference? Can you still do the same expansion and say offer more varieties of chips, but keep the same name?

B) *Extension*

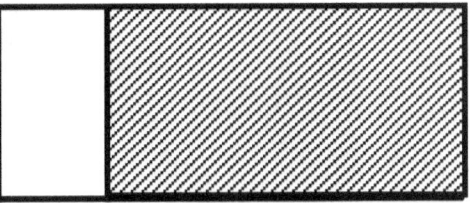

The extension speaks more about the size of the partially change than the other options. An extension means that you take one part of your shops item(s) and make that selection larger in terms of size. Preferably something that already sells well or something you think your customers would prefer that you had more of. The extension would not affect the rest of the shop and you still would be offering the same as you do today.

You may be skipping this one because you think building an extension is expensive and you can't afford it. Think again. Who said anything about bricks and mortar? Many shops who "build" an extension do so by putting up a plastic tent or some other temporarily building. Think about all the tents that pops up in the summer offering flowers, garden furniture etc.

Or do you think that an extension is just for those who own a convenience store? Well, let's play with it for a bit, what could you do if you had a plastic tent, like a party tent? If you are a newsagent you could put in some tables and chairs, offer coffee/tea and decorate it nicely in order to sell more of the "glossy" magazines or more magazines for car or caravan owners. Or what about making the extension itself an attraction? Years ago I went up far up north in Sweden and there was a café who had set up a temporarily extension in form of a tipi/lavvo where you could buy a meal cooked over a fire and eat in the tent as well.

C) *The expansion*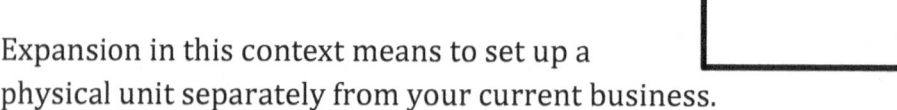

Expansion in this context means to set up a physical unit separately from your current business.

 It will not affect your business or the size of your shop. This unit is not big in size and it consists of high rate in return products and products that are different from what you usually sell. What do I mean with high rate in return products? Put very simple it is just a fancy words meaning you get more money back for each item you sell. How can you play with this then?

Choosing this option it has to be products that give you more money back than your regular products. It can be products that you can buy cheap and sell at a high price. Or it can be products of the upper market, products that are more expensive, higher quality, particular brands or something similar. Do you want it to be one product or more than one as in f. in. a line of products? Does it have to be products at all? Maybe you can offer some expensive services? The products have to be different from your usual stock, but how different do you want them to be? Do you want them to stand out? This is an outside unit, how far outside do you want it to be? Just outside the shop? On the other side of the town, another region? Do you want it to be a stationary, vehicle, permanent or temporarily?

Setting up a unit like this is almost like setting up a new business all- together. It takes a bit more organizing to set up and to run it. You have to juggle a bit extra.

D) *The inclusion*

The inclusion is a tricky one. Not tricky in the sense of being more difficult, but more in the meaning of you have to be more creative. What does this option mean?

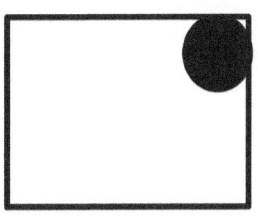

One of the criteria's is that it should be a unit. What unit can you fit into your shop? A unit is a physical object that you can place in your shop without altering the current interior. It also has to be of high income value. It is expected to be a major part of your' total income and not just something extra you offer customers. Last, it should stand out and be different from the rest of your other products you offer.

Like I said, this is a tricky one, so how can you play with this?

Well, if it is a temporarily arrangement you can set up something during the different seasons as in Santa's grotto, summer café, summer flowers. As for what you can put up that fits there are several options. What about a tent that comes in various shapes and sizes? Or small garden sheds or small wooden houses that is meant to be outdoors? Or if you are ready to make a real splash how about a little green-house for the summer flowers or a café, a doll-house, a little caravan offering nail-manicure or a little boat?

Yes, I do meant these examples to be put up indoors in your shop.

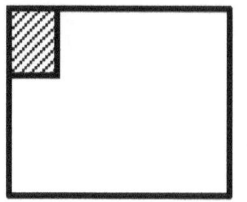 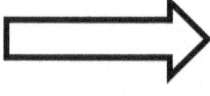 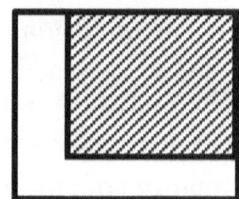

E) *Scaling up*

This is where you notice that one of your products sell really well then you expand that particular product. If it sells really well in the end it could give you the opportunity to change your shop into focusing only on that particular product.

Let's say if you have a little café and notice that your strawberry tart sells really well. You can expand by offering different varieties of the strawberry tart, say different sizes and offer deliveries. You can go all in and offer different versions of it by different types of strawberries, or different berries along with the strawberries. Or you can go for quality by making everything by hand after your' own or your grandmothers recipe. Or you can offer different versions of tarts and pies. The varieties are many and the more details you can find out about what exactly it is about this product that your customers like, the better.

 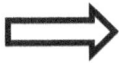 

F) *Flipping it*

Flipping it is where you sell mainly one type of products and have other products in addition to it or in a minor scale, you can flip it around and sell mainly what you now sell in a minor scale and scale down what you mainly sell now.

Means if you are a newsagent and sell mainly newspapers and magazines and offers some different type of coffee you flip it and turn it into a café-bar who offers newspapers and magazines.

You can switch to this option after you tried one of the other and see it sells more than you anticipated and expand in this way with a lower cost without affecting the interior of your shop too much.

G) *Combination*

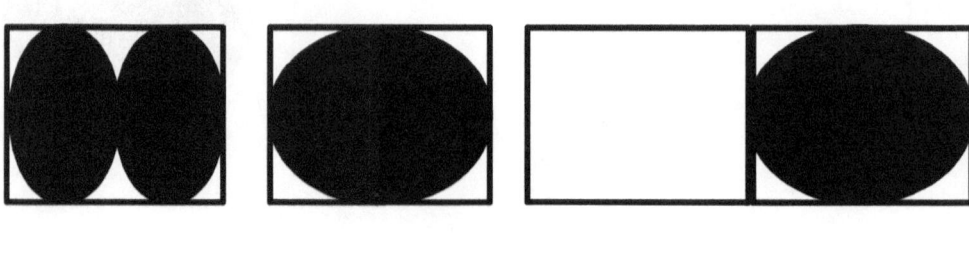

    a)   b)   c)

Examples of combinations:

a) Where the shop consists of two high market products as in watches & jewellery.

It could be the & after the shop name as in handmade leather shoes and Rolexes.

b) Where you turn your whole shop into a high market product – shop and the partially change in this case means the transition-period in-between. Say you turn your shoe-shop into selling expensive brand shoes.

c) Where the expansion is a high market product an you run it as a separate business. Say you have a gift-shop and buy the shop next door and turn it into a beauty parlour, under the same company name.

Playing with this would be to have unusual combinations as in brand shoes and jewellery or how about a beauty-parlour next to jewellery. Or the type of the high-market combination as in if you have one beauty-parlour for women and open one next door especially for men.

Keep in mind that if you put in high market products in your shop as in *the inclusion* and *the expansion* is supposed to be special in some way. If you then offer more of that product be careful so it is not "losing its' magic".

That was a little mental background and you are now ready to work with the model itself. Before you start it is useful to think about how you will organize your ideas. Create a system that works for you that you are comfortable with where you can put information and ideas along the way.

The Fortune-teller Model

Let me introduce you to the *'Fortune-teller Model'*. It is designed to help and inspire you to create your own unique business identity. This model is based on the original fortune teller which is an origami. (If it helps you can fold one of your own and write down the options I use on it.)

First you choose a colour where each colour represents a category. After that you can pick four different ways to use that category to create an identity.

This means you get a total of sixteen new possible business-identities. I suggest you choose one colour and work through that and then when you are used to how it works you can work your way through the other colours.

I recommend that you read through the categories and pick the one that you like the most. If you find it difficult to figure out all the four ways within a category then leave it. You can always go back and make a note on it later. This is about getting inspired and to generate ideas and not so much on getting it perfect.

It is when you choose a category that is opposite from what is natural to choose for your type of shop its get interesting. If you are stuck, try that and see how it goes.

The *Fortune-teller Model* consists of four different main categories:

1. **RED** – Products/Service
2. **BLUE** – Society
3. **GREEN** – The Building
4. **YELLOW** – You

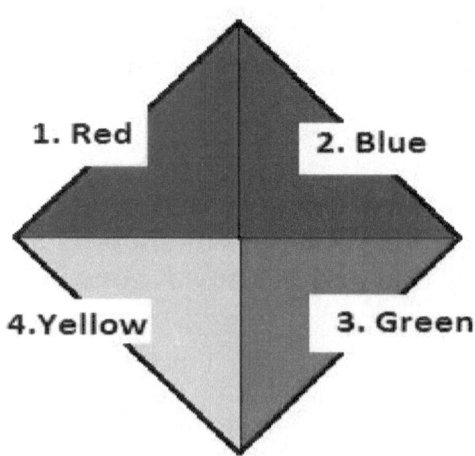

The Fortune-teller Model

RED - Products/Service

Products or Service is where you build it on a specific type of product or a particular type of service.

When you choose to focus on a product or service, keep in mind you are building your business around this. It takes a bit more than announcing now we also have fresh vegetables or to throw in free delivery service. Service here differs from the service in category *Blue -society*. Service here could be a delivery service, but as in courier or a removal firm.

BLUE - Society

Society is where you focus on the society and the people around you. Society can be interpreted in three ways. You can either see it as charity, filling a need you can see in your area. Or you can see it as helping people, caring. Examples of these are day-care, nursing homes or home for elderly. The third way is to interpret it as in being social where people get together. Cinemas, museums and cafés fall into this category and other places or shops that work as a social arena in addition to what is sold.

GREEN - The Building

The Building is where you want to focus on the building itself. You could have an interesting building or a special kind of shop floor you want to show off more. Don't be discouraged if you have an ordinary shop. If you have any interest in decorating or interior-design at all don't be afraid to go for it. This is just as much of what you make of what you got.

YELLOW-You

You here mean where you use yourself as a starting point and what you are interested in as inspiration. You can build it upon something that you have a special interest in or it could be a hobby that you already have you want to develop further or it could be a completely new subject you want to explore. Or maybe the time has come to dig up that secret dream you have. (Any business-ideas you have should involve an element that you, personally, are interested in. Not something you do for anyone else, but for you. If you don't you lose that sense of ownership and it doesn't feel like it is yours anymore. Yes, I know I said it before and I keep on saying it because it is important.)

Four Ways

When you have chosen your category, what you want your main focus to be, you then have four different ways to approach it.

a) Work with what you got

b) Mix it

c) Opposite

d) Go bananas

a) Work with what you got

This is the most common approach. You use your shop as it is as a starting point to find any interesting. Expanding and/or emphasizing what is already existing. This doesn't mean it will stay the same, though.

b) Mix it

Mix it is where you keep one part as it is and mix it with other products or services. This could be to get in same type of products or service, but different or different versions of it. If you have a shoe-shop this means shoes for men, women or kids. Or it could mean working boots, wellies or shoes for special needs. Would it be possible to take in products from different areas, different country or perhaps something produced locally? Do you make something yourself you want to sell? Or do you have a special skill you can offer? Variety is the key-word here.

c) Opposite

Opposite mean you choose the opposite of what you are selling, under your chosen category. It could be to sell the opposite of what you are selling, or the opposite type of your products. If you chose category products/service and sell shoes this could mean selling opposite of what you are selling as in shoes for men/women. It could also mean opposite of where you wear them, say shoe vs. hats? If you have a convenience store say hardware store? Or vegetable-market turning fish-market. Day-care for dogs vs. cats or day- care for kids turning day- care for dogs. How this looks like will differ under the different categories, see the examples later on.

d) Go bananas

Go bananas is exactly that. It is to think unrealistic ideas that you possibly can't implement. Then you narrow them down and adjust them afterwards to something you actually can do and still have that seed of unrealism in it. I know, sounds a bit lofty, but try it anyway. Or you can pick the elements in that crazy idea to use. Think elaborate as in telling a story. First you get an idea then you spin further on it by thinking then what and then what until you have run it dry and can't come up with more.

Including the Remaining Categories

After you have chosen which category you want to focus on and chosen which way you want to use, it is time to include the other three remaining categories you have not chosen. Say if you main category is Products/Service then try to include *Society*, the *Building* and *You*. This is the most important factor in this model. Without it, it can feel like something is missing. Including them in a way that makes sense to you will create a complete business identity that feels whole. When you choose what you mainly want to focus on it doesn't mean that the other parts have to be of the same proportion. As long as they are smaller than your main focus they can perfectly well be disproportionate to each other. The importance is that they are all included somehow.

I know this sounds a bit complicated all this, but stay with me I show you how to use it. Now get that book or sheets of paper and a pencil and set yourself somewhere nice where you can have some peace and quiet. This is first and foremost about getting out of your head and it is about you.

Connecting the Dots

Now that you read the description of the Fortune –teller Model I want to show you how to use it.

RED - Products/Service example shoe/clothes-shop:

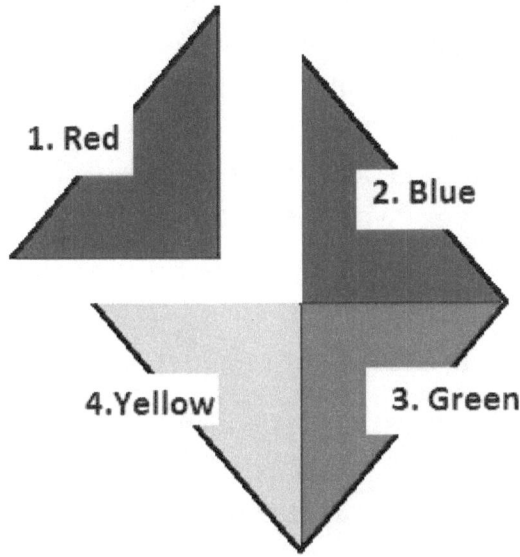

Products/Service is much about taking what you got and enhance it to a bigger scale and to see it in a different light. The challenge here is in thinking bigger and different because this category is the one closest to how you think of your shop already.

a) Work with what you got

Look around you. What catches your eye? What in your opinion is the most interesting item(s)? Do you have any connection to one of them? A story you could tell? I know it is tempting at this point to ask what sells the most. The reason that I don't ask this is because this can change. If you want to build a business-identity around what sells the most at the moment than look beneath the surface and see if you can connect with it personally.

Looking around the first thing that catches my eye would be the newest shoes, especially the one that looks a bit "sassy" and a bit classy. The one that stands out a bit, but not too much and makes you feel nice when you put them on. The other one that stands out would be the wellies and I do have a story about some clogs, but for now I choose to work with the first one.

Including the remaining three:

I choose to work with the first idea which is the newest, a bit wearable fashion shoes. This means including the *Building* that I want to decorate my shop in a bit modern way perhaps for women in their 30's and upwards, maybe put in a nice table and chairs and some magazines to read. Including *You*; I am interested in the latest from New York and London so I would be doing research and background information and to of, course take in the latest, wearable fashion-shoes. Including the *Society* would perhaps be to start a customer research-club where people could come with suggestions to what shoes they want to buy in the shop. It is possible to set aside some space in the shop where the customers' choice would be displayed. It also would be nice if one or two could write background stories about why they have chosen that shoe.

b) Mix it

Having a shoe-shop it is common that you already offer a mix of products, this could be shoes for women, men, kids and clothes. What can you possibly offer that you don't sell already? Any profession you could offer shoes and/or clothes for? Any organizations? Any particular hobbies or interests that spring to mind? This could be fishing, yoga, jogging, gardeners, and nurses to mention a few. What products you choose to add rather depends on what you sell already. Say selling shoes and clothes for yoga enthusiast would not be a problem and would blend in nicely with a general collection.

Including the remaining three:

Including the *Society* in this one it would be natural to contact the specific professions where they work or their organizations to see if the specific group would be interested in a co-operation. Including the *Building* perhaps set aside some space in the shop where they can display their interest and rent the shop to them at half price where they can have courses or meetings. If it does clashes completely it is possible to not use the building at all, but arrange it in a different space all together, say people order online or contact you on the telephone and you deliver it to them. Including category *You* in this one depend on what you are interested in this could be working-clothes for gardeners.

c) Opposite

Again, if you already have a mix of products it could be difficult to see what the opposite would be, opposite of what exactly? You can choose one product and figure out the opposite of that or you can choose the opposite of what you mainly have in your shop. This could be in this case since the example is shoe/clothes shop, hats.

Another version of this could be to go for something completely different, but the same type as in clothes, leads to selling fabric, as in either haberdashery or selling bed-linen and curtains.

Including the remaining three:

Including *You* if I go for hats could be to tell some stories about how we in our family have a thing for hats. Including the *Building* I could turn the whole shop into a haberdashery or I could set aside some space in the shop to display the thing we have about hats. Including *Society* could mean to invite people to give their used curtains and start a sewing club and perhaps invite people to create something as in re-design. Having dressmaking as a hobby myself and some education in it, it would be nice to teach. Do you see how you include the *Society* in your idea determines how you decorate your shop and in some cases it can be proven vital to the whole idea?

d) Go bananas

If you find it difficult to get started you could choose the product that interests you the most. Do you remember where you saw this the first time? Is it possible to re-create that in your shop? Or you could take the product you have the most interesting story about. Is it possible to create that story in your shop? Can you find inspiration from magazines? If you really are stuck try to listen to some children or ask them. Another way is to listen to the news and see if one of your products is mentioned in a funny story. For me it could be to recreate the convenience store where I got my first clogs (You could get everything in those little co-ops.) Or it could be creating a shop around wellies in all colours, shape and sizes and selling rain-gear. This to try to recreate the feeling I had when I was a kid and splashed around in the ponds.

Including the remaining three:

Including the *Building* of, course the shop could be decorated in various bright colours and the obvious customers would be families with children. It rains a lot where I live and coming from an island and having a grandfather that was a fisherman, well, somehow I have gained a lot of experience about rain-gear. This would be what rain-wear and wellies would work in what type of weather and for what purposes so I suppose it would be natural for me to including *You* by being the one who picked out what to sell in the shop and to whom. Including the *Society* it could be fun to start a fond and organize a wellie- run for charity.

Key Points

RED- *Products/Service*

Choosing this category and *a) work with what you got* is perhaps the most common approach. It is a risk that it still can be a bit anonymous. Thinking bung in a few tables and chairs, order more of them fashion boots and decorate the shop a bit fancy then you are all done. The trouble is everyone can do that. You have to have a reason why behind it. If you struggle with the identity, work on getting a solid why.

For example:

-What if the product that caught your eyes were the shoes for kids, a little pair with pink flowers on. Can you think of your first shoes? What is the first pair of shoes you remember? Why? What did they look like? How can you facilitate so children can get the same feeling, what other products/items would go along well with it? How can you help customers tell their own shoe-stories about their first pair?

Can you picture what this shop would look like? At least you have an idea where to begin. Isn't it easier when you get the why behind it?

If you don't have any interesting stories then ask around. Ask older relatives, ask younger. Get the stories behind it.

Try to figure out how you want to include *Society* in your idea at the same time. It can be vital for how your idea and your shop are shaped.

BLUE - Society example Convenience-store

Perhaps it seems a bit odd to choose category *Society* for a convenience- store, but if you think about it all shops are arenas where people meet in one way or another. The shop and you serve your community more than you might think.

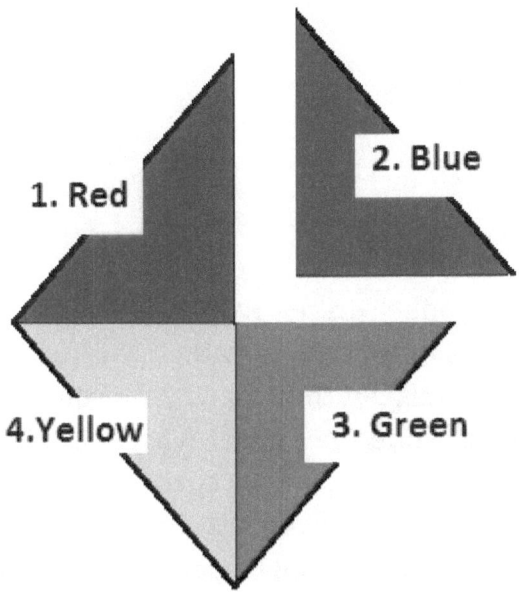

If you are an owner of a small, village shop you know this already. Even when you are a shop in a high-street you are not anonymous. How your shop is, affect the others.

a) Work with what you got

Keeping in mind that this is under category *Society*, take a look at your shop. Is there are need in your area that can be filled with the products you have? How can you encourage people to become more social using your current products? Can you facilitate anything in your shop? Using convenience-store as an example in this case the obvious answer is starting a soup kitchen. Another version can be to sell food that is out of date, damaged, or engross in large quantities; cheap.

Including the remaining three:

As you can see what products to sell gives itself when you figured out your main idea. The products follow the idea. The shop has to be fitted to the idea as well, but think of ways to complement it even more. Perhaps set aside some space where people can eat or ways to display or arrange the food in a special way. Your role in this scenario could be to enhance the fact that some food gets better the longer they pass their sell by date such as certain cheese. Also perhaps hold courses or make information available on how to make most out of your food, you know, '*waste not want not*'.

b) Mix it

Mixing it in this case could be to keep the shop as it is, but adding a social element that is equally amount in either proportion or in importance. This could be if you set aside some space in your shop for darts-matches, or start a bridge-club that meets in your shop. It could mean to set up a space at the back where you can teach how to mend lawn-movers if you have a hard-ware store. Here I would have chosen to either start a cooking club or hold cooking classes at the shop using ingredients from the shop. What you do, what type of club or in what shape or form this takes, rather depends on what you are interested in. It is connected.

Including the remaining three:

The question here of course is should you focus on products you already got or to get new ones for this new club or courses of yours? Both, I say, but begin with adding products that is connected to the new club or courses you starts. Then let it dribble into the rest of your stock of what you offer if it is a success. How much of your shop you want to set aside to this is up to you. You could either set aside some space for it in your shop or you could arrange it next to it or at a completely different place entirely, but make it clear it is arranged by your shop. The category *You* in this is already included since it is connected to what you set up.

c) Opposite

Choosing the category *Society* when you sell products is already going opposite. To balance it out you can keep it under the same parameter as you are in so it has that same familiarity. In simpler words it means you either keep something as it is or you have something as a reference to what you do now so people can recognize it. It sounds more complicated than it is. In this example it could be to turn it into a smoothie bar/café and keep the current name and still sell what you are selling now in addition. Or it could be to keep the interior as it is, but turn it into a museum telling the story of either your shop or the story of the old convenience stores in general.

Including the remaining three:

Here again you see that the idea gives direction to the rest. What *Products/Service* you sell follow the idea. It also depends on how much you want to change your shop. Choosing the first idea, the smoothie bar/café you have to change it completely. In the second at least you get to keep the interior as it is. In this one your role is different in the two. In the first you get to use your creativity when figuring out different types of smoothies. In the second you would be more of a guide.

d) Go bananas, dream

Do you have any favourite TV-show, any TV-program you like? What makes it your favourite TV-show? Why do you like it? Any favourite places you visited? Why do you remember it? Any tournaments, shows, gatherings, and fares you like? Any persons you find inspirational? Here it could be Master Chef and those bake off competitions. You could use the idea as it is and turn the shop into a master-chef kitchen, keeping the interior somewhat as it is. (Sort of, it probably would have been some legal issue involved regarded the brand name and so on.) Or you could perhaps install a kitchen in attachment to the shop and make some cakes to sell and set in some tables and chairs? And hold a domino-tournament? Or you could invite people to bake with you in the kitchen, perhaps elderly who sits alone much of the time. Or start a grandmother/grandchild baking club for those who don't have one? I mean older people without grandchildren and kids wanting a grandmother/father.

<u>Including the remaining three:</u>

Including the *Building* would be to install cooking facilities of some kind. *Products/Service* would be anything that has to do with cooking or baking. Probably best to choose one of them. Including *You* in this could be making cakes or meals yourself to sell or as a teacher holding courses.

Can you think of any talent you have that would be natural to incorporate this way? You do, I can assure you, you have. If you feel embarrassed about it perhaps another angle could be to think of something you would like to learn, together with others and let someone else facilitate it in your shop.

Key Points

BLUE – *Society*

Figure out the main idea first then work with how to include the other three categories.

What products to sell give itself when you figured out your main idea.

It is easy when you say social to think of clubs and memberships, but these are more products that follows the idea. They are not enough as a business identity idea.

Also think about this:

-How involved do you want to be?

-What role do you want to play?

-What would YOU like to do?

When you have figured out what role you want to play in it, what you want to do, it gives direction to how the idea is going to be.

Meaning as in the idea of installing a kitchen do you want to cook and make products to sell, cook with others, teach or hire out the facilities.

Choosing *Society* keep in mind that you have to make money out of it as well, especially in the long run.

GREEN - The Building example Gift/Card- shop

Here the point is to make the building or the shop itself an attraction, to give people a reason to visit mainly for the building. I wanted to use gift/card- shop as an example because it is a bit anonymous.

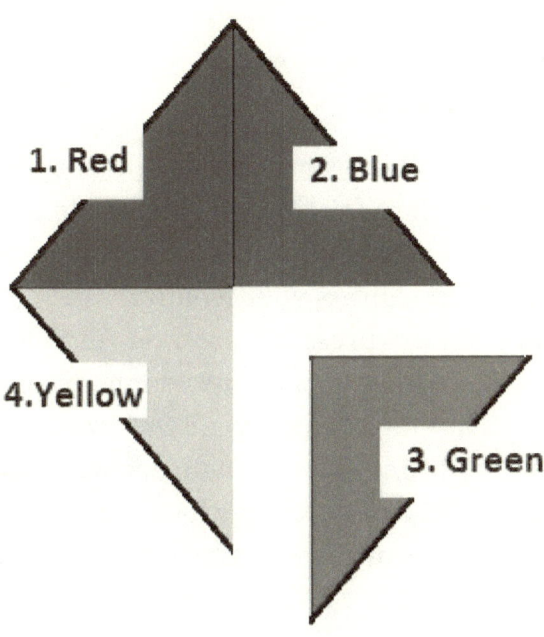

a) Work with what you got

Working with what you got here means you use your current products as a starting point and an inspiration. Think of it as in how can you make your building reflect your products? In this example it is a gift/card- shop so here it can be to decorate the walls to look like a giant gift-card.

<u>Including the remaining three:</u>

The products are already there since you use them together with the building. To include the *Society* think of when do people send cards? Can you give people a new reason for sending one? Sending cards is a way of express your feelings, can you think of other ways to help people express themselves? Here it could be to set aside one of the walls in your shop for people to come and write messages on as a remembrance wall. Or it could be to install a fireplace (or a symbolic one) in your shop and set up a place where people could come and write love letters to the one that got away, to those they daren't send it to, to those who never will be and burn it in the fireplace up the chimney as a symbol. What is your relationship to your products? In an idea like this the bond between the building and the product gets very strong. Together they become the dominant factor and your role in it is almost only as a facilitator and what you add to this has to strengthen the whole idea. Here it could be if you make personal post-cards.

b) Mix it

Mix it under the *Building* means you decorate your shop to fit your current products as in the example above and keep one part of your products as it is, but split it so you change the other half.

Including the remaining three:

How you include the *Society* here help you choose what products or service to take in. Gift-cards can be used to express emotions and it is used in different occasions. And in different occasions we are in different moods. Think of an occasion, say birthdays, what mood are you in? What can help you get into that mood? When thinking of birthdays the first thing that springs to mind is birthday hats and other props. Thinking of what put you in that mood can help you to come up with other products to sell. Here this can be candies and lollipops in various colours. Keep in mind that it has to complement the remaining products and the building. It could be seasonal, permanent or it could be a service or some sort. Your role in this is connected to the complementary product or service. Here this could be to make the lollipops, hold courses in the shop and offer a birthday-arrangement service with products from the whole shop.

c) *Opposite*

Going completely opposite here means you flip-it. Flip-it is where you take the products that complemented your current ones in the previous example and choose to focus your shop around that. Leaving your current products to serve as complementary product instead. Follow this here it would mean to decorate the building into a giant lollipop and sell handmade candies. If you don't like your idea for the complementary product in the last one you can always change it. Think of what your current products would serve well as an accessory to.

Including the remaining three:

One of the products that are going to be sold it is known already, the current one that is already there. Then there are the products that follow the complementary product, which is now the main theme. Here it is the candy. Then there is the combination of those two which makes up a third and it is here you can have some fun. It could be to sell lollipop with gift-cards, *say it with a lollipop* and have them delivered to the one you love and so on. Including the *Society* and *You* in this goes together and it is hinted at before, handmade candies. This could mean to hold courses in it, to invite people to make them with you and then sell them in the shop if they want. It could be to set it up as a birthday activity with kids and to hold more in-depth classes for those who want it to take it to another level.

d) Go bananas

Do you have a picture of this shop in your head? The giant lollipop outside, the smell of the hand-made candies inside and the colours? Now think of the sweet-shop in Harry Potter and transfer it to this shop, what would you add? How about a little train, a gigantic spinning lollipop, open up the attic or make one if there isn't, create all the little nooks and cosy, exiting spots and having little work-shops?

Including the remaining three:

What on earth to take out from this one? You could either adopt the whole idea as it is and try to re-create a sort of Harry Potter sweet-shop universe. Or you could take one piece in it and use it as it is, as in copy and paste, put a train in or open up the attic. Or you could use the concept and thoughts behind it as in creating more movement and excitement, to evoke that sense of discovery and adventure. Not necessarily it will bring new products in, but if it does they will be complementary products and add to the mix. The idea is to strengthen the identity of your shop. If you go for the Harry Potter sweet –shop how can you make it more like that?

KEY POINTS

GREEN- *The Building*

Here it is much about getting good at reading your building. When you practise that, you get better at determine what idea and product would be a good fit, or not. Equally important though is to tell a story with your building.

What story do you want to tell?

When you choose this category it is better to work with all the four ways at the same time. You might have seen that they are connected and works better if you look at them as a whole idea. The idea changes gradually from the beginning to the end. If you don't like the idea or want to change your role in it, it is better to change it in the middle; fig. 2&3

1. *Your shop and how you decorate it*

2. *Products you currently sell*

3. *New complementary products*

4. *New, different looking decorated shop*

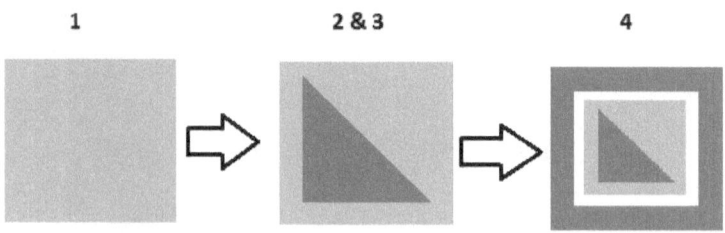

Learn to read the building

Reading the building is not as mystical as it sounds. It is about looking at your building or shop floor to see what would be natural for it. Is it an old building with a typical periodic interior or a new, industrial appearance or is it a neutral, modern and non-personal office space type? What kind of slates, what colour, texture and so on. It gives you a starting point to work from. Whether or not you follow it you can decide later, but at least you do it consciously. Many say that if you are not sure then go for a neutral colour, but that is not necessarily a good idea. It has to match what you are selling too. You don't expect to have white walls and metal chairs in a Mexican restaurant do you? And by the way, that's another thing. The interior and the colours have to match. Both with each other and then with what you are selling. When you do this try to forget about what you want to sell, for this is about the building and your space. Afterwards you can see what you can sell from what it has turned into. If you find this difficult do some research by take a look around. See if you can find a shop in a similar building to yours and see what they have done. Why you like it, why you don't and what is not adding up. It took me a while to figure out why a convenience store was confusing. They had placed the check- out to the right so you entered the shop from the left. Others had them placed to the left so you entered the shop to the right. (Many have done it like this because it is said it is more natural when you are right handed that you instinctively want to turn to the right.) What you also can do is to keep this in mind when you are out shopping in general and see what they have chosen to do, if you feel something is off, try to figure out why. If you have an old building or a building typical for a specific period, ask experts or someone who knows the history behind it. The idea is to get a background and objective views.

Do you have any interest at all in interior design, architecture, re-furbishing or decorating?

Then go for it, even if you feel your shop-floor is a bit anonymous. It won't be after you put your touch on it.

YELLOW - You example Newsagent

You here mean you use yourself (and your interests) as a starting point for creating ideas for a business identity.

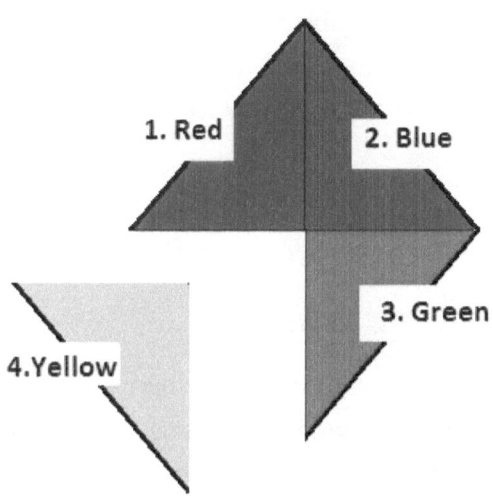

a) Work with what you got

Take a look around you at the items in your shop. What catches your eye? Why? Any product you can become a specialist in? Anything you have an interest in? Any of your products you can tell a story about? A haberdashery I know has a very friendly owner and on one occasion I went there he told me an amusing story about how he required some white buttons with yellow flowers on. Years later I still think of those buttons and the shop.

What magazine or newspaper stands out to you? Why are you interested in it, why do you like it? Is it the stories that they tell? The products they sell? The way they tell it? Or the photographs?

Is it possible to echo it in your shop somehow? Is it possible to sell more of the same type of magazines or newspapers?

Do you struggle to find anything that you are interested in?

I know this is going to sound daft, but it is possible to have your own shop full of products and you don't like any of them. Don't push yourself to like anything. If you don't find anything of interest then try to think about what type of product you are missing. Here, what magazines or newspaper do you wish you could sell? Is it possible to require it?

Or, how about starting up a newspaper yourself?

Including the remaining three:

Let's say you are interested in magazines for women. Including the *Building* could be to decorate the newsagent as a newsagent for women. Including *Products/Service* could be to think about what type of women's' magazine do you like, is it fashion, gardening, for younger/mature/career women? What other products or services would the type of women like? What products to offer could also be to sell the same type of products in the magazines. The *Society* could be included by setting up a blog or a newspaper and invite different women to write in it. You could set up a chair or a coach with a computer and let them come in the shop and write.

b) Mix it

What products in your shop do you like and what products would you like to replace?

Maybe here it could be to keep the magazines and throw out the newspapers. Then you could expand the magazine part. What is left then is to replace the newspaper bit. You could choose to go digital with the newspapers and let customers read newspapers on e-book readers, or Ipads in your shop. Do you want to keep everything as it is and find something different to add to your products instead? Then perhaps services are something for you.

Services tend to be forgotten a bit, but are just as valuable. Do you like to ride a bicycle? Or do you enjoy reading stories for others? Then you could offer a service where customers can buy newspapers or magazines and other goods from your shop and you deliver it with your own bicycle. Or you could offer to read out loud from the newspaper to say elderly people.

Including the remaining three:

What other products can be sold or read on these e-book readers? What other ways can you use the new product you added? Including *Products/Service* could here be to sell e-books and newspapers that only are online. Or you could make your own weekly podcast about the news. You could offer a service where you buy the fee for online newspapers and customers could come to your shop and read it for free. Then you could sell coffee/tea and perhaps a snack to go with it as well. When you offer more than typical delivery service then the service is a type of product itself when you make a bit more of it. Make a splash with the service itself. Give people reason for wanting that service other than it is free or fastest.

Including *Society* could be to offer a membership or where you invite people to suggest what e-books or newspaper to sell. Make a competition where they write their own e-books and the winner get to sell it in your store, (Setting up a web-site with an online store would be preferable here.) And let the winner read out loud from it in your shop.

You would have to adjust your shop to fit these new offers and with these adjustments where you sell more magazines and online newspapers and e-books it gives it an overall modern look. Including the *Building* could be decorating it to be more modern, crisp sort of look. Or you can go the other way by making it a contrast; give the shop a really old, look.

Another way to include the *Society* here could be to split it into a delivery part and one for reading out loud to others and hire someone to do it. Some may want to only deliver and others may only want to read out loud for others. You could hire kids with their own bikes to deliver and elderly to read out loud. Or someone would like to do both say a parent with a baby-buggy to deliver and read out loud. Put an item in your shop that reflects what type of services you offer. Say a kid's bike or a baby-buggy with a sign on it describing the service.

c) Opposite

Describe a day at your shop and what you do. Done?

How much of it is routine tasks? All? How much of it do you enjoy doing? If your answer here is nothing then it is time to do something about it. Try to see what tasks you can streamline and what you can do without. What you can get someone else to do and put a time-limit on the rest. It can't be all tasks that need to be done, at some point you have to take care of customers.

Do you like talking to customers? What do you like to tell them (apart from telling them to sod off.)? What would you like to talk to them about? Would you liked to show them something? If you find it draining to talk to customers then what about setting up more self-service? Or do you like working on displays? Or do you like to make it all comfortable and lay it all out for the customers to enjoy it?

Try to find something that you enjoy *doing*.

Can you see the clues above? First is about storytelling, the second is more design and the visual, the third is about giving people an experience.

Including the remaining three:

Storytelling:

What would you like to tell your customers?

What would you like to talk to them about?

What other ways would you have liked to tell a story?

Here the example is newsagent so it can be the latest news, the weather or politics.

Including the *Building* could be to decorate the walls with newspapers from all over the world and use items that says news and have a TV with a news-channel running in the background.

Products/Service could be to sell more newspapers and other in-depth, newspapers.

Including *Society* could be to put in a table and chairs where you could sit and talk about the latest or if you prefer, you could set up a camera and interview people what they think about the latest news. A form of coach-TV.

The important bit here if you like storytelling and talking to customers is to set it up to facilitate it. Think about ways that can help you to talk with customers. You have to have something to talk to customers about. Certain items perhaps can help you getting started.

Design and visual:

If you like the design and visual then make the shop itself a design feature. Use the whole space in the shop, including the ceiling. (And outside if you can.) What is it about the design and visual you like? Is it the colours, the way it is set up or the lines? Think about new ways to show the items in your shop.

What other ways can you express your interest in design and the visual?

Including *Products/Service*

Could you make a product yourself to sell? Here it could be a magazine or another item you have made.

If you can't think of another similar product then perhaps another item that could be an aid to the products you are selling.

Or it could be a service, aiding and showing the customers how to use items.

If you are interested in design and the visual is a lot about how it looks and making it look sleek. A service here could be to help them to do what you do. (Decorating, putting outfit together, organizing, colour schemes, visual art to mention a few.)

Including *Society* could be to offer to hold courses in your shop or to get in touch with a school or open university that have courses in what you are interested in an offer to facilitate them.

Experiences:

What experiences would you like to give to the customers? And don't say a good experience because that is too vague. If it helps you could try to think about what feeling you want to give them. Glad and up-beat? Exhilarated and thrilled?

So, not scared and terrified then?

Including the *Building* would be that it reflects what feeling you want the customers to get. Happy, sad, reflective, scared and so on.

Including *Products/Service*.

What else could contribute to give them the feeling you want? What other items gives them the same feeling?

Including *Society*.

Do you want to play a part in the experience (as in storytelling) or do you merely want to facilitate it and let them experience it on their own.

In this newsagent example it could be to dress up as a witch/wizard and tell horror-stories at midnight.

Or it could be to put in a giant teddy-bear and tell bed time stories for children. Let people bring their own favourite bed-time story book and read out loud from it.

Or how about combining the two? Ask people to write horror bed-time stories for adults and read from them in your shop?

d) Go bananas

Isn't it strange how we tend to bury those dreams and put them in a mental draw with the label stay in there? We create that mental divine that says that dreams are meant only be just that, dreams and then we turn back to reality. Now take a deep breath. This is about opening up that draw again and taking a look at them.

Do you have a project or an idea that you always wanted to try out and see how it goes?

Do you have a dream of changing career? Is it possible to try it out in your shop by combining the two?

If you don't exactly dream of a different career path haven't you sometimes said to yourself that you wished you could test out a different profession for fun?

If you don't have any career or profession you want to try out you can try this approach instead.

This is more about creating a new daily life so describe your dream-daily life. How would a "normal" day look like?

What part of you do you wish you could use more often in your daily life? What part of you do you miss using?

Do you have any hobbies or interests that is typical you?

Why did you start the shop?

How can you design your shop so it reflects you and who you are as a person?

What would it take for you to step into your shop in the morning with a sigh and feel at home?

None of these are easy questions and it may take a while before you can answer them. Let it. Give yourself the time you need to think.

A little word of advice, try not to involve other people at this stage. Others can have a strong opinion on what you should and shouldn't do and what is typical you. This is about you and you know yourself and your shop best.

Having trouble going bananas? Let me help you.

This is about you, going bananas and in this case a newsagent.

Right.

Want to be a journalist? Start your own newspaper/magazine and turn your shop into a "news-room" while still selling what you do now. You could also hire others to write for you.

(If you sell shoes/clothes and want to be a tailor or a designer then turn your shop into your own show-room and work-space.)

What am getting at is make your shop into your very own play-room and set up your own work space where you can work with what you want in peace. If you are scared of making such radical changes to your shop then this is all still on paper remember? Allow yourself to at least play with plans.

<u>Including the remaining three:</u>

You may have some sort of idea what this is going look like.

Including the *Building* by making space for your own work shop or change the whole shop itself to fit the new newspaper. Let the newspaper or magazine you want to start be in focus. Put in a desk or two or couches if you prefer. This is about you and your taste. Put the newspapers and magazine you currently sell on a rack on the walls and the rest of the other items in a corner, for example. Let it reflect you.

Products/Service is of course your new newspaper/magazine in addition to the rest of what you are currently selling. But what could you add to the mix?

Of, course you could sell other office supply, coffee/tea and other snack. What could you sell in addition that you like yourself? Or what items says you that you could sell?

For me this would be to sell my own photographs, coffee with hazelnut blend (or moccachino) and my own pastry.

Including *Society* could be to hire local people to write for you or give them their own column. Ask local people what they would be interested in. Use local people as sources for information and as experts.

KEY POINTS

YELLOW –You

In *Yellow* you incorporate you in the business and use yourself as a starting point for ideas for creating a business identity.

You begin by adding a little bit then it gradually builds up to the last idea where you have a business that it reflects who you are, that says you. (Like knowing who you are as a person when you walk into your shop.) *You* in this case do not necessarily means to enhance you as a person, though of course you could change the name of your shop to match yours. This is more about where you get to use more and more of your interests and who you are in it, something that is so easily forgotten and difficult to get back.

-What items are you *interested* in?

-What products do you *like?*

-What do you *like doing* during a day?

-What do you dream of *being?*

Did you notice that the two first are about outer interests such as products or what you are doing. The last two are about who you are as a person.

Adding that Extra

Nearly finished, but before you dive into dissecting the ideas it is one last thing. By now you have four different ideas if you have chosen one category or sixteen if you have worked your way through all of them. Adding that extra is about adding a surprising element or a twist that lifts up your idea to a new level.

You can do this by playing with the what, where and for whom.

I am using the first category as an example.

RED - Products/Service example shoe/clothes-shop:

a) Work with what you got

Looking around the first thing that catches my eye would be the newest shoes, especially the one that looks a bit "sassy" and a bit classy. The one that stands out a bit, but not too much and makes you feel nice when you put them on.

<u>Including the remaining three:</u>

I choose to work with the first idea which is the newest, a bit wearable fashion shoes. This means including the Building that I want to decorate my shop in a bit modern way perhaps for women in their 30's and upwards, maybe put in a nice table and chairs and some magazines to read.

What type of customers springs to mind when you read this? Can you picture them? What do they look like?

Are they blind? Do they use wheelchairs? Do they like to hike? Or interested in theatre?

b) Mix it

Having a shoe-shop it is common that you already offer a mix of products, this could be shoes for women, men, kids and clothes. What can you possibly offer that you don't sell already? Any profession you could offer shoes and/or clothes for? Any organizations? Any particular hobbies or interests that spring to mind? This could be fishing, yoga, jogging, gardeners, and nurses to mention a few.

What products you choose to add rather depends on what you sell already. Say selling shoes and clothes for yoga enthusiast would not be a problem and would blend in nicely with a general collection.

What about pets? Clothes for pets or combining them say for yoga and pets? In this one you can play around by choosing an unusual club or organisation to co-operate with. Say the local cycling club, hiking club or riding club. Not unusual enough? What about motor-cycle enthusiasts; run by elderly? Or classic cars? This means you can take your shop out and about as well and sell at shows.

c) Opposite

You can choose one product and figure out the opposite of that or you can choose the opposite of what you mainly have in your shop. This could be in this case since the example is shoe/clothes shop, hats.

Another version of this could be to go for something completely different, but the same type as in clothes, leads to selling fabric, as in either haberdashery or selling bed-linen and curtains.

Including the remaining three:

Including Society could mean to invite people to give their used curtains and start a sewing club and perhaps invite people to create something as in re-design.

How about kids? Teenagers then? Create a sewing-room where they can re-design clothes. Or someone who has a dream about being a designer let them use your space and sell what they created in the shop. Or move the entire concept of re-design where to as say, nursing home or hospital.

d) Go bananas

If you find it difficult to get started you could choose the product that interests you the most. Do you remember where you saw this the first time? Is it possible to re-create that in your shop? Or you could take the product you have the most interesting story about. Is it possible to create that story in your shop? Can you find inspiration from magazines?

To add that little extra here the interesting part is the story behind it. Not so much changing what you already offer, but changing the backdrop sort of speak.

Ask local historian, visit museums, and search the newspaper archives. Look through magazines and videos. Can you see if your products is displayed anywhere? Who is wearing them, in what setting? At barbers shop? In an old fashion cowboy-movie? In a romantic black and white movie? Or a movie from the 80`ies?

Combining all four into one idea.

Another twist you could try is to see if you can combine all four ideas into one.

 -How about re-design to 80'ies sports-gear to the local disabled-sports-club?

-Or re-design to historical hiking gear to the local hiking club?

See how it shifts the whole idea?

Now that you are all done I'll ask you again

What is unique about your' business?

Pick one of your options and try to answer it.

Describe your business. How do you feel?

Aren't you a tiny, bit proud of it?

Evaluation

Now you are done with the idea stage it is time to look at them with a more objective eye and evaluate them. Before we even start I want to stop one of your thoughts. That thought that says *I don't need to go through an evaluation I know what would work or not just by looking at them.* That thought alone can stop you from looking closer at all of your ideas and by that miss out on what you actually can do.

Another is one you most likely hear from others.

How many times have you heard that it isn't practical? It is a sentence often used to shoot down ideas before they are looked at. What does it even mean? This is what the evaluation is about. In reality it means you go over your ideas one by one and take a look at what practically needs to be done to implement them. When people use that sentence that it isn't practical often they haven't looked at what it actually takes to do it. It is more that they are intimidated by the idea and it feels like it is too big and too much. Remember it is you who do the evaluation. Don't let others shoot down your own ideas. If you *feel* it is possible find out what *practically* needs to be done even if others say it isn't possible. Break it down into the major parts to begin with, too much details makes it overwhelming. This could be interior, suppliers, what do you want to sell etc.

The third trap is to choose the idea that fits best with what you got already. I know it is easy to think like that and it is a difficult one to avoid. It is natural to slide towards the one that demands least effort to do. Also when it fits with what your business looks like at the moment it feels like the right one.

You got four ideas with that added extra and one overall general idea from all of them. Write them down if you haven't done so and keep them next to you. Copy or fill out the evaluation form as you work your way through the set of check-points to see which one is worth working further with.

Recourses

It is easy to think of money when you think of recourses, but here the word is used in a wider term including equipment, skills, people *and* money. Recourses are more a question of how you can get it done. What and who can aid you? How much change is necessary before you can implement it? Is it something that you can start working on right away; do you have the equipment needed already or does it require radical changes before you can get started?

Go through your ideas and see where you could encounter some major difficulties. What would be the snag in the daily running of it? Is the snag minor or major?

Is it an expensive idea? Are there some elements in it that makes it too expensive that you can exclude or replace or is the whole idea itself costly? How can you make it cheaper?

Who do you know that has skills that can be useful to that idea? Can you learn the skills yourself? Who do you know that can help you with the lifting, carrying and organizing? What can you sell right now that would give you money? How much time would it take before you can make money out of your idea? And last how much money do you have, if anything, to spend?

Go through your ideas and give a score from 1 to 4 where one says it is an expensive idea, that you or anyone you know hardly have any of the skills needed to finish it and it is difficult to get the equipment to do it. And four is where it is a cheap idea (or you know how to get it cheaper), you have almost all the money it takes, that you and the people you know have the skills it takes or you know how to acquire the knowledge to accomplish it and you have most of the equipment needed in place.

Market Assessment

Market assessment is where you try to figure out if it fits into the current market. How on earth do you tell if it is a good idea or not? What you are wondering about is how to tell which idea will give you the gold at the end of the rainbow. Well, I give you an answer and you are not going to like it; it depends. It depends if your idea meet a need in the market, at that current time. There is however some questions you can think through. Is it a new idea, a novel one or an old have been done before idea? Is it popular? When did it become popular, a while back, a year back or very resent? It is good if it is a new idea, but not if it is too out there. You know your local area best and you know how they will react. Will they say, hmm and be curious in a good way or will they think, oh that's a bit too freaky? What does your local area need? What do people miss? Could any of your ideas fulfil that need, if yes that is a plus. Are there any shops in your local area, county or country even that has a similar idea and makes money? Can you visit them or look the up on the internet to find out how they make money? What do they sell, what do they offer? Is it possible to do the same with one of your ideas? If yes, that's good.

Go through your ideas and score them from 1 to 4 where one it is an old idea, you have many competitors that do the same thing, or it is a really novelty idea, or it is difficult to figure out how to sell it practically, and it is hard to see what need it fulfil. Four is where it is a fairly new idea or an old idea with a new twist, you can tell which need it fills and you don't have that many competitors or there are shops with a similar idea that makes money.

Describe it as a person

Think about your business in terms of a person and not as an object. Who is it? What does it do? What personality does it have?

If you have trouble choosing between the different ideas, go for the one that you can best describe as a person. It would be a lot easier to build up a business around that idea. Maybe you think this is a bit ridiculous, but try it.

A positive side-effect of this is it makes it easier for you to market your products and your shop. Customers connect better with a shop that has a clear identity. You know who they are and what to expect. It also helps you to develop a marketing plan since you know what type of people you are aiming for. Ask yourself these questions: Who is similar to your shop's person? Who wants to hang out with a person like this? Who wants to be like this?

Choose one of your ideas that you like and after you tried to describe it as a person try to invent a background story about this person. Or better still, try to talk to someone who is similar to the person you are thinking of. If you are lost, try to spot a person you like and think of how to make your shop into a personified version of them.

Go through your ideas one by one and try to describe them as persons. How easy is it to describe the idea? Do you get a picture in your head who it is?

Give your ideas a score from 1 to 4 where one is where you struggle and it is scattered and difficult to grasp and four it is easy to describe and you get a clear image of who it is.

(Under the column *Person* in the *Evaluation* form.)

You

Did you notice how easy it is to lose yourself in the equitation? When you adjust your ideas along the way it is easy to adjust yourself and what you want out of it because it is not that important what you want, is it? How wrong can one be? I can't stress it enough how important this is. This is actually the most vital part of all. If you don't get to do something that interests you in your business you lose the sense of ownership. Having lost that it can be difficult, in some cases impossible, to see the point of it all. Your enthusiasm is one of the best marketing tools you have. Look through your ideas again and see where you fit in them. What do you see yourself doing? What role would you have in the running of it on a daily basis? How interested are you in what you see yourself doing? How much of your strengths do you get to use in it?

Close your eyes and picture yourself in the daily running of your shop once you implemented this idea, how do you feel? Do you feel strong, enthusiastic? Or weak and depleted?

The feelings you have now when you think of that idea, those feelings are the one you will carry around with you when you have implemented it.

Give your ideas a score from 1 to 4 where one is where you do about the same thing you do now or you feel weak, depleted or rubbish. And four is where you have a new role, get to use whatever talents you have (or want to develop) and you feel strong and enthusiastic.

Value factor test

After you given them a score you hopefully have a better overview of which ideas that have potential and which is better left on the side. An interesting thing though is if you do a vector test. A vector test is roughly that you put a set of inputs provided to a system in order to test that system. Sounds complicated, but it isn't, really. Here the vector test is a value factor. Up until now the five headlines have been given equally importance. Meaning a 4 under Recourses is just as important as a 4 under Market Assessment. A value factor test means that a 4 under the headline you find most important weighs higher than a 4 under those of less importance. It can complicate things, so instead we are going to use a much easier way. You simply take two of those headlines that are most important to you. Then you add up the score of those two and put it in the Value Factor Score in the form.

Look over your ideas again and do this test with this in mind. Does anyone stand out? You can get ideas that scores high in your value factor test, but have a low score in the other. If you have an idea that you really like and score high in the value factor test, but have a low score in the other you can try to even it out. Let's say that two of your highest value factors are *Market Assessment* and *You* and one of your ideas scores high on those two points, but have a low score on the *Recourses* and *Person*. What you can do then is to work more on those two categories to get the overall score higher.

The Evaluation Form

Idea nr.	Recourses	Market Assessment	Person	You	*Score*	*Value factor Score*

Give each idea a score between 1 and 4.

Don't let others shoot down your own ideas. If you *feel* it is possible find out what *practically* needs to be done even if others say it isn't possible.

Project Planning

Making a project plan is exactly that, a plan how to implement your idea. This is where the idea transforms into something real.

Maybe you have done something like this before, if so that is brilliant. If not it can feel a little daunting. Before you panic and get overwhelmed with the thought of planning a big project I am going to break it down for you into steps. A simplistic version of project planning you can follow. For now this is just to play with the idea of going through with it. Mainly to help you think things through and get used to the idea of changing your shop.

This is only a brief overview. If you want to know a bit more about planning a project you can read on further in the next headline *'Project Planning Details'*.

Take a look at your list and pick two ideas that you want to work further with.

Which two ideas have the highest score?

Which two ideas have the highest score in the value factor column? Are they the same? If not you can pick the one that has the highest overall score and the one with highest score in the value factor column.

Description of the project

Write down a description of the project. Write a short introduction of it. if you like you can give it a name. Here you can also write down why you think it needs to be done and what you think it will do once it is done; both for your business and for you.

Practical implementation

What actual work needs to be done? What changes has to be made to the shop? In what order does the work need to done? What needs to be done first? Do you want to have the shop open during the work or do you want to close it for a short period and then re-open or do you want the work to be done at evenings/night after the shop is closed?

What major items need to be purchased before the work can start? What new products do you want to buy to sell in your shop?

What would you have to do with the products you are already selling? Can you sell it along with the new items you plan to bring in or do you plan to have a completely new line of products?

How do you want to go through with the shift? A big sale on all the existing products and then in with the new one? Or a bit smoother transition by introducing the new products little by little?

How would you make it coincide, the work done in your shop and the shift in your products you sell? Do you want to bring in some of the new products while they are working? Or do you want to wait to bring the new products in after the work is done and then open with a big bang with a new shop and new products?

Financial overview

What would the material cost? What would the major items cost? Can you get it cheaper? If so how and how much cheaper? Do you have to hire professionals for the work, how much would that cost? Or can you do it yourself?

How much money would you lose during the transition?

Time-frame plan

This is a big one. If you struggle to guess a reliable time-frame for this then ask professionals and ask around. Ask companies; ask others who have done something similar. And remember this; it always takes longer than you anticipate.

If you need to hire professionals for some or the entire job, then it is best to set up a time frame after you get their quota. Then you see how long they anticipate it takes to get the work done. Sometimes you need to negotiate to get a time frame to get it done in time.

Laws and regulations

Any specific laws that apply for what you want to do? What about import/export laws and taxes, how much would it cost and would it be expensive?

Also check out what you are allowed to do yourself and what work you *have* to leave to the professionals.

What is the biggest obstacle with this project? Perhaps it is an emotional one. Even so it should be taken just as seriously. Many times it is not that it *can't* be done that stopping us. It is that we *feel* we can't do it.

After working through this with your two ideas I suggest you take a break because your head would be spinning by now.

Choosing Idea

You may find after this that it either takes too much time, it cost too much, you can't get people to do the work, it is impossible to get hold of the products you want to sell or that there are certain laws that put a stop to it.

If you still find it difficult to choose then ask these questions and see if it helps:

-Which idea is closest to your' heart?

-Which idea is closest to your ethical values and which one, if any, clashes completely?

-Which idea do you feel ready to do?

If you can't choose between the two of them, then don't. Stick with the two for now.

About when

I suppose you expect me to say that after you have been able to choose one idea then go ahead with the more detailed project plan and well, do it. Yes, eh, no. There is such a thing called timing.

The different business identity ideas have perhaps grown on you and you feel ready to go ahead with it. Great, that is quite an important part. If you don't feel ready to go through with it then the chances are the project is going to strand is very high. But even if you feel ready that doesn't mean that the environment will follow. Meaning you start the work on your project and then it all fall into place. Work *with* the surroundings instead and wait until the pieces fall into place and *then* go ahead and start with your project. It all sounds a bit mumbo, jumbo, doesn't it so I try to explain.

You may have heard some business-gurus talk about having that hunch and you either got it or you don't. This is a crucial point because I think you have many great ideas in you, but you hold back when it comes to implement them. And what makes you hold back I can guess, it is that nagging doubt and the uncertainty for what would work and wished you had that hunch to be more confident. Sure, there are some that is born with that special hunch, but they can't come over and run your business for you, nor should they. Let them bang on about that hunch and then train your own instinct you got in you. You doubt you got one? I don't, you know why I know this? Because you use it already in other areas of your life. Still sceptic? Think back about the last time you bought a bigger object, this could be your car, TV, bed or a freezer. You didn't go straight to the shop and bought the first thing you saw did you? Not without a rough plan or idea of what you wanted anyway, right? How did you know when it was the right time to buy it? And how satisfied were you afterwards? What did you get right and what did you got wrong?

 Put it all together and this is called hunch.

In front of you, you have the rough outlays of the two ideas. You know what it takes to go through with them, you know what work needs to be done, what items to purchase and so on.

In the weeks or months to come, keep the implementation plans for your ideas in a place where you can easily reach them. What you do then is to keep your eyes and ears open to see if anything occurs that is related to one of them. That law or regulation that prevented you from going ahead with it is abolished, the new products you wanted to sell is popular, the items you needed to purchase is on sale etc. One is great, two or even three is definitely a signal that the time is right. The more that is lined up the better.

Project Planning Details

As promised here is a bit more about project planning.

Description of the project

Yes, I know, I know, it is the same thing as the one before. Her it means going into more detail and being more precise. What is it that is going to be done? Why? Not so much I feel this and I want that, but more exact and specific.

Also put down the preferred start date and when you see this project finished.

Categories

After you written the description you have some idea of the major tasks that needs to be done. See what major categories you can divide the work into, such as interior work, decorating, stock, items, marketing. There are two methods to use when you divide the project into categories. You can either use something called a function- oriented structure or you can use an action- oriented structure. The first is used when there is high risk and uncertainty. One task is finished before the other starts. In the action-oriented there is more certainty of what needs to be done and the smaller projects within the project overlap.

Try to think of them as this; in the first think in terms of substantives and in the second action- oriented think in terms of verbs. It is common that these two overlap and my advice is to choose what works best for you.

After you have divided the work into categories you can dive into each category and figure out what needs to be done within that category.

It is after you have figured out what needs to done within each category you can see with more certainty what type of project it is; if it is a function-oriented one or an action-oriented one.

Ask these questions:

-Does one work needs to be finished before another can start? For instance the carpenter needs to do its job before the electrician can fit the lamp.

If so, in what order does in need to be finished? What needs to be done first and what comes last?

-Can the work within the categories be done simultaneously?

Follow up

Have you heard of something called *Gantt diagrams*?
It is a method developed by *Henry Gantt* around 1900 to plan and measure progress in projects. It is quite simply a chart or diagram where you fill in the planned activities and how long you anticipate it takes to do them. When I say simple I mean that literarily.

Activity \ Durance	Project week #			
	1	2	3	4
1. Knock down walls in shop	▬▬	▬		
2. Fit new lights		▬		
3. Decorate the shop			▬▬	▬
4. Order new products	▬			
5. Marketing campaign				▬▬

(Obviously you know a lot more about what it entails to do this.)

After you contacted suppliers, carpenters etc. you have a more accurate idea of how long the activities are going to take.

Critical path

Critical path is defined as: *"A chain of activities that combined makes the longest durance"*. (*'Project- organisation, management and implementation'* By Bjørn Johs.Kolltveit and Torger Reve, Universitetsforlaget)

It is the critical path that decides the length of the project. I could go on and on about this and put in more calculations. Let's say that is all about focusing on the critical path and shortening the length of it. In an event of success in doing so then another critical path might emerge. Simple right? I try and simplify this and make this less complicated (said the pot to the kettle...). The definition of the critical path means to take a look at your project and see what you think is going to take the longest time. Is it the plumbing? Does it involve some major construction work? This work is not done in one big operation. First you have to knock something down, then lay foundation, concrete, plastering etc. What they mean is how can you get that done faster. Personally I think this is a lot of cobwebs. Firstly you don't know how long it is going to take until you get proposals from in this case professional constructors. Plural, I might add, because the offers vary. Some say it takes fewer days, other says it takes longer to get more money. The answer is somewhere in between. Second, putting all focus on the work that takes longest time, well, then the other activities would come second wouldn't they? Aren't they just as important? Of, course they are. The importance doesn't come into it. Only the calculation of the time it takes to do it. *Thirdly, what looks like it is going to take the longest time doesn't have to be the one that actually does so in reality.* Instead try to monitor each category as equal important. You know at what date or thereabout, the individual categories need to be finished and that is most important.

Practical advice

At last I want to give you some practical advice regarding projects based on experience.

If you have your own method to plan and get an overview over the project, then use that no matter what it says in a book, (mine included.) As long as you have the overview that's all that matters.

There will be some that wants to overcharge you and there will be some who drag things out to get more money out of you that way. Spending some time up-front before you start the project can save you a lot of money and headache. Ask for offers from more than one contractor and ask others who have used them to get an idea if they are reliable or not. And please, do get a fix contract up front for the work all-together and not on a per-hour basis. It saves you from unpleasant surprises later.

There also will be some who interfere and question the entire project and wants to decide and make changes, without asking you. Keep it in mind when you hiring.

Staff quarrels are one of the reasons a project is delayed. It is not irrelevant who you are hiring.

Figure out what motivates people. Not many take a job only because it pays well. Setting people to do something they are interested in is a good chance to lower the rate of quarrels. Apart from lowering internal conflicts, wages cost money. How many can you afford to hire? Do you want to outsource the different categories if so, how many and who will do the others? Do you want to have people being in charge for a category or do you want one assistant to help you throughout?

Be clear of what task people should do. Not so much in detail, but more of what they are responsible for and what the expected outcome is.

A project is going to take longer than you think, cost more than you think, there will be delays, there is going to be some last minute hick-ups and something will go wrong so you have to improvise. And when you are about half-way or so into the project there is a dip in motivation, both for those who work for you and yourself. Be aware of it up-front and plan for treats and motivations.

Don't expect a project to go smoothly. It is not a failure if it is bumpy and chaotic, that is the very nature of a project.

Then if everything goes alright it will be a nice surprise.

And oh, yes, good luck.

A word at the end

Changing your business is never easy. You have to face your fears and your doubts of your own abilities. Not to mention the lack of hope and the mistrust from others. This on top of all the practical challenges you have to deal with. This is my attempt to encourage you. I am trying to say that you can trust yourself to make the right decisions, that you are capable enough to do this.

This book is about easing you into the idea of change and hopefully you have gotten a few ideas that is interesting. Now what? It is so easy to forget about ideas, put them in a drawer and close it for good, but I rather you did that then nothing at all. Between thinking and doing lies a huge gap and thinking new ideas is a start. When you get used to the idea of changing your business you can pick up those ideas again from the drawer and take it from there.

Have you ever thought reading this book; *why on earth did she thought of that or that is a daft idea, why didn't she suggest this instead*? Good! That is exactly what I hope you do because that means you have kicked those creative brain-cells of yours into gear. This is *your* process, *your* ideas. My ideas are not better than the ones that you come up with, they are merely a reflection of my own thought process through this. As yours will be of yours.

So, when is the right time to start working with your business identity? The right answer, if there is any, is whenever you want to. No, seriously, the answer is it is better to start with it when you want to and not when you have to because everything is going pear-shaped.

Are the days of the small shops over? I don't believe so, but their role in society has to change. They have to become a part of the society and fill a need that is more about what they are selling. Your shop is more important than you think.

Personal Notes

2

{ 3 }

www.ingramcontent.com/pod-product-compliance
Lightning Source LLC
Chambersburg PA
CBHW030702220526
45463CB00005B/1870